Welcome to the Museum of a Life

Previous Poetry Collections,

Magnifying Glass
(2020, Black Eyes Publishing UK)

Vortex Over Wave: Photography meets art meets poetry
(2023, The Daydream Academy)

Welcome to The Museum of a Life

Sue Finch

Black Eyes Publishing UK

Welcome to The Museum of a Life
© Sue Finch, 2024

First published in 2024
Black Eyes Publishing UK
Gloucester
United Kingdom

www.blackeyespublishinguk.co.uk

ISBN: 978-1-913195-26-7

Sue Finch has asserted her moral right under the Copyright, Designs and Patents Act, 1988, to be identified as the author of this work.

All Rights reserved. No part of this publication may be reproduced, copied, stored in a retrieval system, or transmitted, in any form or by any means, without the prior written consent of the copyright holder, nor be otherwise circulated in any form of binding or cover other than that in which it is published and without a similar condition being imposed on the subsequent purchaser.

A CIP catalogue record for this title is available from the British Library.

Edited by: Josephine Lay

Cover: Jason Conway, The Daydream Academy
                www.thedaydreamacademy.com

For:
my sister and all our museum adventures;
my wife and that dropped pound coin;
and all those on my poetry path.

Contents

 9 **Foyer**

11 Gallery 1

13 A Garden Pond
15 When I Saw Jesus in a Tomato
17 Digging that Hole
19 She Puts on a Spring Dress the Day the Tortoise...
20 You Told Me Ladybirds were Carnivorous Beetles...
21 Pelting
23 'Clambake'

25 Gallery 2

27 Silence
29 I Hate You
31 Wolf
33 Dropping Your Baby
34 The Peacock
35 Untitled (Portrait of Dad) *after Félix González-Torres*
37 I Don't Know
38 Preparing the Wedding Flowers for Delivery

39 Gallery 3

41 Scruffy Jack *after David Berman*
43 My Hybrid Heart
45 Telford's Warehouse
46 That Coin
47 We Few Deified We Few

49 Skating
50 Hopscotch

53 Gallery 4

55 Tuesday Night
56 An Apple for My Mum
58 Invitation
59 Hanging On
60 Acceleration
61 Rescuing the Giraffe
63 Blade
65 Last Night I Dreamt I Slid My Poems into Drawers…
66 Jars

69 Gallery 5

71 Deathwatch Beetles
72 Overnight
73 Do Geese See God?
74 A Pelican is Dancing on the Patio
75 Blackbird
77 I've Nothing to Offer the White Horse…
79 Do You Hear the Helicopters?
80 When I Am Gone

83 Museum of a Life: The Unexhibited

85 Gift Shop
87 Acknowledgements
89 Sue Finch
91 Full Quotes

Foyer

*On entering this Museum of a Life,
visitors are free to move amongst the galleries at will.
However, we would suggest that visitors should begin
at Gallery One.*

Gallery 1 – A gallery of childhood

Enter this Gallery to see:

a dog blanket,
a large home-grown tomato,
a spade,
a photograph of Fred the tortoise,
a book, open at the nursery rhyme 'Ladybird, Ladybird,
Fly Away Home',
a shed window with spiderless cobwebs,
a Ouija board.

A Garden Pond

I had never seen so many shades of darkness.
Difficult to distinguish
dark brown from burnished black.
I was happy there
staring.

My reflection stared back
rippled.
I wanted to kiss it.

I already knew there were countless versions of green –
pure lime green
dark army green
fairy tale frog green
the endless mixing in of yellow.

A snail with an algaed shell
moved as if in outer space.
I was close to gripping it.
Then I was right in there
amongst bouncy pond weed,
straggly ribbons of leaves
and those shades of brown and black in close-up.
Oh, the depths of it.
I was so cold amongst the stale green smell
but happy.

They shouldn't have ripped me from it
just to wrap me in a stranger's dog blanket.

Rough wool held me silent
all the way home.
The air had chilled me to the bone
grey dog hairs stuck to my lips.

When I Saw Jesus in a Tomato

I was at my nan's
and there he was
rocking to steadiness
in a halved tomato
next to a rough cuboid of cheese.
When I showed her, she nodded
murmured affirmation
but I wonder did she really see him?
Maybe her eyes were like mine are now.

I ate him;
he was a woody version of grass.
I swallowed him hard
not wanting him to get stuck
in my throat.

No phones then to capture the moment
only a headline in my mind.
When I returned home, I told my mum
what I'd witnessed.
I think perhaps she thought I was lying
or had conjured him from my imagination.

Months later, I worried them all:
nan, grandad, mum, brother.
Quick spit it out.
Get it out of her mouth! I heard
as the grown-ups stood in horror.
They'd watched me

bite through the first glass
I had ever been allowed to use.
All I knew was
I'd been staring at the new wallpaper
making crucifixes from the repeating squares.

Digging that Hole

Day after day she let us dig that hole.
You made the sides straight
marvelled at lines you called strata.
I just liked the way there was real orange
in amongst the expected brown
how it looked sliced instead of dirty.
I disliked the crumbs at the bottom,
that never diminishing scattering,
that I couldn't spade out.

You said if we kept on, worked hard enough,
we'd feel warmth from the centre of the earth,
that we'd know by laying our hands flat
on the bottom of our freshly dug hole.
You told me Australia was right beneath us.
It all seemed so worth digging for.
I pictured us emerging in a different country,
staying there until teatime,
coming back to tell Mum.

Each time you pressed your palm to feel for heat
you looked hopeful
silently inviting me to copy.
But I only ever felt the cold damp
of earthworms.

The first thing I thought of each holiday morning
was digging that hole. I pictured you
spade ready, jumping in, getting started,

swinging your loaded spade high.
I imagined myself up top
remembering that those excavated piles
took up more room out of the hole than in;
shovelling the earth away as quickly as I could;
being interrupted by your sudden warning –
it's hot, the lava's coming.

She Puts on a Spring Dress the Day the Tortoise Comes Out of Hibernation

She sits with him on her lap

dips cotton wool into the bowl of water
balanced on the arm of the settee.

Gently and slowly, she works to unstick his eyes
trying to mask the fear
that he is not going to wake up

that he has been dead all this time.

We watch
not knowing which will fascinate us most.

When the flicker finally comes
he empties his bowels
on to her lap.

We are impressed that all this comes
from such a small creature.

She sits unmoving, as the puddle,
now larger than the tortoise itself,
begins to seep through her dress.

You Told Me Ladybirds were Carnivorous Beetles that would Bite My Fingers if I Picked Them Up

And yet I saw you
whisper singing
as one walked the length
of your index finger.
You were pointing it to the air.
Hushed tones
as if you were the one
who had set its house on fire
just to watch it
break open the crisp shining red
to unhinge the grey, net-curtain wings
and rise.

Pelting

The single thud-thump
that signalled death
still sounds in my chest sometimes.

A brown rabbit
with unquestioning eyes
being carried in
on a rainy day.

Stress makes tough meat
so hands as big as haunches
stroke it to calm
on the wooden bench.

I swear
there are whispered words of love
as ears are folded back
to reveal the soft white fur
at the nape of the neck.

As the stick is raised
I am held by the silence.
Through the cobwebbed window
I still watch.

Those eyes die within seconds
then the back legs are tied.

I cannot remember how long it hangs
how long before the blood stops dripping
from the quiet nose
how long before fat fingers push in
to separate pelt from flesh.

I just know I hate the rip
and the peel
and the thought of those hands.

'Clambake'

Some say it was one of his worst movies.
The night its title was spelt out
in the tiles on the Ouija board,
I'd not even heard of it.

The question lingered on the air
like smoke from a blown-out candle,
Is there anyone there?

My thighs clenched, dreading a reply.

A pause then
before the spelling began

E – L – V – I – S
and then Presley
as if the surname was needed as full proof.

I loved Elvis –
those movies with the helicopters
his quiffed hair
the songs
the way the crowds went wild
while I sat, unmoving, on my settee.

Which of your movies was your favourite?
Such a waste of a question.

So many things we could have asked
when, of all the people calling on the dead that night,
he chose our glass to slide across the table.

Too scared to make a sound I waited,
watched that slow movement to the letter C
before the frenzied zigzag to complete the spelling.

I wanted to ask if he was happy.
And if he was
why was he in our living room?

I could never drink from that glass again.
Each time I slid the cupboard door open
I forced myself to check
it was upside down.
Every day I wanted to smash it
to set the ghosts free.

Gallery 2 – A gallery of the unspoken

*Enter the gallery
to the sounds of a dawn chorus.*

Inside you will find:

*taxidermy models of a heron and a wolf,
an unclothed doll,
a green grape,
an installation of Félix González-Torres's mints,
a bureau filled with tea and sugar,
and a box of wedding flowers.*

Silence

Silence stands in the hallway all night
says she doesn't need to sleep.
In the morning, she is in the chair
waiting.
Sometimes she smiles
and I think she gave me the dream
about meeting Dolly Parton for the soundcheck.
Sometimes she is so aloof
I imagine she sent me the handless mob
lumbering towards me
bloodied boxing gloves
where fingers should have been.

She has birdsong in her;
sends the call of a bittern
to make me laugh
after she has taken me to the darkest silence.
Once she tapped me on the shoulder
at 3am, handed me the car keys
got in the car with me
and directed me to a forest.
She took me over a stile to the darkened path
where we could not see our feet
and the bumps and gnarls of roots
sat under the mud.
Before my eyes adjusted
she stopped me, stood with me
to hear the last owl
and the first blackbird.

Once she wrote me a note
folded it, put my name on it
so that she could watch me open it
and read, *I am your shadow.*
Her drawings tattooed the page –
a tarnished axe
a coffin
and a holly bush
all its leaves on the ground.

I Hate You

said the cow.
Yeah, she hates you, whispered the grass,
hates you,
hates you, it swished on and on.

So, I climbed the gate.
Get off, you're too heavy, said the gate.
Yeah, you're gonna break us,
said the padlock on the chain.

I stepped over a large muddy puddle
marvelled at a greeny-brown cow pat.
Imagine creating that!
Then I remembered that the cow
hated me
and I ditched my admiration.

Stop looking at me
and notice how quiet it is, stupid,
said the cowpat.

I lifted my head to the clouds
caught the eye of a bird I couldn't name
saw its beak begin to open.

I wondered if the silence would shatter
like a pint glass, all splinters and nibs,
or just quietly split down the middle
like surface ice on a pond.

There's only one of you.
The unknown bird was staring at me.
I waited for it to cock its head.
It remained still;
a totem carved in the tree.

You want me to repeat that
don't you?
mocked a heron
standing on the path,
You think I have ancient grey wisdom
and the key to solitude.

I did.
I wanted to keep going
but as his wings opened like a prayer
I froze.

Wolf

After the first time
she smelt blood all day.
Even pacing for hours
in the cold air
would not let her lose it.

The second time
it was on her tongue
and in her throat;
spoonfuls of cream
would not carry it down.

After the third
she learned to soap and irrigate
her nostrils
her tongue
each of her fingerprints.

She was ready
to grip her own knife
to listen to the rip and slice
of the wolf's belly.

She imagined feeling; the skin give way
the slit expand
that soft puff of warmth
the scent of his guts.

Holding her breath
she pushed stone after stone inside
let her hands slip
in the warm, thick red.

The blood dried stiff on her hands
before she sewed tight criss-cross stitches
to seal him dead.

Dropping Your Baby

If you drop her when we are paddling,
I promise to fish her out of the sea.
I'll pass her right back to you if she falls
from your hands during an autumn walk.

But if you throw her out of the car window,
on that awkward roundabout where the A5
takes us closer to the M54,
you won't get your baby back.

And if you dangle her by the ankles
then let go on the QEII bridge,
even if all the traffic is stationary,
she'll remain face down on the road.

I won't retrieve her
from anywhere in the Dartford Tunnel,
or be able to get her back
from the bottom of Bishopstone Glen.

If you throw her into the pond in the park
I might not be able to hand her back.
In fact, she'll not be safe anywhere
if you sling her in a temper.

And I won't keep handing her back
and handing her back
even if the sun is shining
and the leaves are beginning to fall.

The Peacock

Do you remember the peacock
that ate the grape
that rolled from our picnic?
How we were amused at first
by the swollen oval
in its neck?
Then shocked by how slowly it sank.

I remember swallowing hard
wishing that would help
and looking into its eyes
wanting to know if it was panicking yet.

It stood stately, unblinking,
before taking ballet steps across the grass
its head back and to
searching for other things to peck.

Do you remember us going back later
to check it hadn't choked?
Us hugging each other in sheer relief?

Untitled (Portrait of Dad)
after Félix González-Torres

In the far corner, against a white wall,
a metre wide pile of mints
half a metre high
and the title: "Untitled" (Portrait of Dad*)*.

I am halted by wrappers
stuck sticky-tight to striped mints.
I'd have liked them cool and refreshing
not buttery
not body-warmed, offered in hot hands
from trouser pockets.

One sweet for each day of a father's life
tokens of love with unspoken words.
Artist says: *I like people to play with my art,*
so, I sit down in the pile of wrapped mints
eat one and pocket two.
Then I start to shape the edge, curving it
to resemble the mouth of a conch shell.

I picture Grandad leaning on the wall
at Neptune's Jetty;
cap on, eyes to the horizon.
I replay the scene,
walk towards him smiling,
knowing he'll dip his hand in his pocket
and this time I will take the humbug.

Artist says: *I like people to play with my art.*
And that invitation to touch
had me eager up all the flights of stairs.
A man is talking into a walkie-talkie
heading straight towards me.
Artist says: *I like people to play with my art,*
yet this is not allowed.

I am escorted from the gallery;
my lime-green jacket
watched down every stairwell.

I Don't Know

I don't know exactly how many seconds there were
between your final two breaths.
I don't know if anyone else in that room just thought
we would be watching and waiting forever.
I don't understand the impurity of mixed fruit jam.
I can't know if you died hungry or thirsty,
grateful or knowing.
I don't know if biting one by one
through a dozen budded tulips would help.
I don't know if you really thought people
come back as birds.

Or whether it was your way of keeping the dead
alive. Not having to say goodbye.
I don't know how seasick you were
on all those cruises you took for him.
I don't know if someone has your bureau
in their house, if it still smells of the tea and sugar
you stashed inside for years.
I can't know how cold you were with no heating.
I don't know if always wearing a vest,
a jumper and a cardigan helped.
I don't know what it felt like when you undressed
for bed.

I know your cheeks were cold wax in the chapel of rest
that you looked peaceful and beautiful and young
that I wanted you then as a statue
so, I could keep you with me forever.

Preparing the Wedding Flowers for Delivery

On Monday
I crush the stems.
On Tuesday
I rename the orders.
On Wednesday
I pluck off the outer petals.
On Thursday
I store the boxes in a heated room.
On Friday
I pull out all the white roses for my own bouquet.
On Saturday
I steal them all.
On Sunday
I place them on untended graves.

Gallery 3 – A gallery of love

Enter this Gallery to see:

a scarecrow,
a copy of 'Gray's Anatomy',
an artist's impression of 'Telford's Warehouse' in Chester,
a pound coin from 2002,
plated fiddlehead ferns (help yourself to a free recipe card),
a pair of ice-skates,
a hopscotch grid,
an oil painting of a sparrow held in cupped hands.

Scruffy Jack
after David Berman

What does he do? you ask,
when I tell you to salute
and say good morning.

He collects the prayers from the crows, I tell you.
Why? you ask.
So they can fly lighter, I say.

You look up at me.
I will my mind to think faster
as you ask, *What do crows pray about?*

The same as us, I tell you,
rapidly scanning my brain
to recall the last time I prayed.

My prayers were always for the sick;
desperate words followed by promises
I'm not sure I kept.

You tug on my hand to get my attention back.
Would I be light enough to fly if I gave him my prayers?

No, I tell you, *human lightness is different,
it's a feeling, like when you are so happy
you are floating on the inside.*

Oh! Like when we squashed the worm casts on the beach before anyone else was awake, you say.

We continue to stride across the field.
Behind us the scarecrow stares straight ahead
the wind tickling his roughly stuffed-in hair.

I am grateful for your silence
and the hugeness of the ocean in my mind.

I do want to tell him though, you continue,
because he is God isn't he, if he collects prayers?

My Hybrid Heart

I put my fist slightly off centre on my chest
draw round it, with red marker pen,
make a Valentine's heart.

It needs to be bolder.
I outline it again
with black.

I recall the pages of my old *Gray's Anatomy*;
add in a fat aorta
ventricles, atria
forget where the vena cava goes.

I leave it out
press lightly to feather in the valves
laugh when they look like ghosts.

If I still had the book
I'd check to see what I'd missed
but I am happy
with the hybrid I've created.

Once, I had an echocardiogram,
its peaks perfect
despite the fact it felt as if you'd tied
rough brown string round my heart
and pulled it tight.

Connected to that machine
I tried not to think of you
didn't want to feel adrenalin daring me
to breathe fast.

What would you say if you could see me now?
Call me crazy?
Ask me if I had nothing better to do?

I look in the mirror
meet the lines around my eyes
with a flirtatious smile.
This could be my first tattoo.

Telford's Warehouse

It's uncanny how I was
pulled there twice;
once by blue ink
once by a choice of tea or beer.

It's uncanny how I can see the bridge so clearly
yet thought we were invisible.
How the man in the alley
shocked me when he looked at us and said,
I have seen you before, you are lesbians.

How little sleep we got that night.
You had to ask me where we were
when you phoned for a taxi
in the morning.

It's uncanny that what kept us awake
was fast hands and tongues
wanting everything
from every angle
as if hours were threatening to speed past.

It's uncanny
how when you told me you had a date
with a beautiful woman the next evening
my heart fell.

That Coin

I imagine putting that pound coin in my mouth
tonguing it from heads to tails
and back again.

As you walked in,
a clock somewhere struck eight,
while the minute hand of the one I was eyeing
clicked its thirtieth tick.

Your hair
your skirt
your make-up
your eyes straight ahead
told me
you were out of my league.

Then that fumble of fingers
had that coin falling from your grip.
Your one flaw was all I needed to say my name.

Like a one-armed bandit on triple seven
I rattled out the stories of my life

and still you said yes to a coffee I wouldn't make
and paused on the bridge over the canal
to kiss me.

I could love that pound coin forever.
Take its metallic tang again and again.

We Few Deified We Few

Wanting us to feast differently
I filled a basket with fiddlehead ferns
right to the brim for you:
ostrich fern, lady fern, bracken.
Tossing their bitterness
with garlic and rock salt.

Look, I tell you, *I have foraged
this taste for you.*

I let lemon zest fall on
those curled caterpillars
amongst the charred green-brown leaves.

We do not mention
that vague muddiness on our tongues.
We do not mention,
amongst the charred green-brown leaves,
those curled caterpillars.

I let lemon zest fall on
this taste for you.

Look, I tell you, *I have foraged*.

With garlic and rock salt
tossing their bitterness:
ostrich fern, lady fern, bracken.

Right to the brim for you
I filled a basket with fiddlehead ferns;
wanting us to feast differently.

Skating

I watch her
skating straight out across the ice
taking a furious 'here to there'
zigzagging a line.

No laying down of tight circles
no figures of eight
dizzying on her frozen pond.

I swear I see thoughts
thrown out above her.
I watch them dropping slowly
through the fir trees.
Sometimes I see them right up against the sky
she can make them touch that blue.

There's so much she wants
to outrun
leave behind.

One day she will let me skate beside her
take her hands
show her how to spin.

Hopscotch

The numbers should be in a straight line
like a road, or left to right
with a zero at the centre.

Hopscotching them is wrong
it's not even that the odd ones make a
pattern for your feet to land on.

You say I should be throwing a stone
to tell me where to jump to
that just going from one to ten
is not how it's done.

I don't tell you I am only doing it
because it's there
or that I think using a stone is wrong.
I like the smoothness of dice and counters
the satisfaction of rolling fair-weighted ones.

It worries me that the squares aren't square
and what of the chalk with its impermanence?
I fear I cannot hopscotch with you.

It's ok if you don't want to play,
you are saying, *I understand.*
But I don't want you to understand.
I want you to change the game;
adapt the rules
and make it better.

I'll play, I tell you,
just don't make it stop at ten.
Make it last longer.
Make the squares as square as you can,
go to one hundred,
and find me the smoothest pebble possible.

We can't use a stone if it goes to one hundred,
you tell me
as you pocket the chalk.

Gallery 4 – A gallery of dreams

Enter this gallery to see:

a blue apple,
images of shooting stars,
an inflatable ladder (do not attempt to climb),
accelerator and brake pedals,
a giraffe,
a blade fashioned from ice,
drawer set containing poems in disinfectant,
a large exhibition jar.

(If you'd like to have your photo taken in the jar,
please ask a member of staff for assistance.
We cannot be responsible for unauthorised access.)

Tuesday Night

She puts down her drink
says she has something to tell me.

I am counting the seconds of her pause and breath.

She says she is afraid
that a bird will die in her hands
that there are things in the world
she cannot save.

I ask her how many birds she has ever cupped
she tells me none
but says, she's seen them held.

I ask her how many
of those carefully cradled creatures died.
She is silent.

I do not know the words to reassure her.
I worry that offering to hold these dying birds
will not be enough.

An Apple for My Mum

I need to tell you exactly what colour it was.
Did you ever suck an American boiled sweet –
a blue one –
slip it out of your mouth
hold it to the sun to admire it
before sliding its smoothness back in
and licking the wet sugar coating from
the pads of your thumb and index finger?
It was nearly that blue.

And did you have that gel toothpaste
so bright you squeezed it the full length
of your brush's bristles
even though you knew the tube
said 'pea-sized'?
The kind that had you wondering how blue
made teeth white?
It was almost that kind of blue.
And it shone like the first strokes from a bottle
of nail polish labelled 'electric blue'.

And there it was
hanging from the branch of a tree
within reach
and no one had picked it.

So, I got it for her, that bluest of apples,
and all the way to her house
excitement held my stomach captive

as I imagined her biting into it
or wanting to put it on display
for the whole world to see.

Invitation

Just as I am worrying
that I cannot read binary –
she says I will be able to see
Perseids tonight in her armpits.

I assure myself I can Google it later
hoping that the instructions
will be simple.
I plan to have a notebook
and pen ready.
I know that joke about
there being 10 kinds of people in the world:
those who understand binary
and those who don't.
I tell her it would be great
to see the meteors up close,
nuzzled right in.
*They don't make your neck ache
this way,* she says,
*and you will be able to hear
the crackles of ancient fires –
it is all deep in there.*

I wonder if we will ever be
sociable again after this.
How many people in the world
are hankering to see
night skies in the armpits of lovers?

Hanging On

Sure of the rope that had me swinging
certain the rungs were wooden
I thought of the grip of past climbers.
All the dirt pushed into the twists
smoothed and darkened
by person after person.

And here I am
three-quarters of the way up
suddenly swaying on unanchored plastic,
with the realisation that the ladder is inflatable.

I cling on;
tell myself height is irrelevant
that I was ascending before.
Say that, if hand over hand
worked a few feet in the air,
there is no reason to doubt it now.

I will the sway to stop
keep listening.
I go faster
desperate to outclimb that gentle
puff of escaping air.

Acceleration

I did not waste a second
flooring that pedal
getting it firm on rubber matting

yet I am accelerating
backwards.

I have never been this fast.

A straight road taunts with cartoon endings:
a canyon to fall in
a brick wall to hit.

I am sure I could not
press the brake any harder
yet I cannot stop.

All my strength is standing down.

Rescuing the Giraffe

I count the tangled legs; make it six,
one head, so I count again.
This time I make it a knotted four
its eyes are fixed on mine
as if I was its mother.

But how do you retrieve
a giraffe from an earthquake crack?
And then what do you do with it?
The trees are bare
and I feel unqualified
for this emergency act.

I am sure its skin will feel like suede
and those hot chocolate eyes implore.

You are a poet, you owe me this, it says,
so, I sit on the edge
reach down my hands
pat its gentle rump.

It is all muscle under that thin, soft skin.
I stroke tentatively.
Don't bite me, I say,
and the giraffe is offended.
OK, what I mean is
it might be uncomfortable
while I sort out your legs.

It barely makes a sound as I work.
Released feet scrabble to find their place
on the jagged sides of the hole.
It is ready for the haul.

My arms cradle its stomach,
leaving the legs to dangle,
and I have him rising.

He is as unsteady as the day he was born;
skidding like a skater on their first rink.
But finally, he is up,
shaking off confusion
and I am seeing the size of our shadows.

Blade

I fashioned a blade from ice; carved its purity
with steel – ran with it to the circus tent.
I raised it above my head
so it flashed under the lights.

The slow drip down my wrists
reminded me this treasure was temporary.
But I'd made this and the moment was mine.

Too early for the ringmaster and clown
to be in full costume; braces dangling
cheeks pink
faces not yet settled
they breathed grassed air and watched.

Are you auditioning? asked the ringmaster
breaking the enclosed silence.
I felt sure I could pull something off
but wondered how I'd cope in the cold caravans.
Was it time to see so much more of the world
or had I carved this beautiful dagger
for a different purpose?

I frowned thoughtfulness.
Then, feet together,
I lifted my melting weapon above my head.

Neck back
I opened my mouth as wide as I could,
tasted yesterday's popcorn tinged with hotdog,
slid it slowly in.

I am 98% sure they applauded.

Last Night I Dreamt I Slid My Poems into Drawers of Disinfectant to Sterilise Their Titles

Today a poet in black stands at a lectern
reading her words.
At the end she straightens her pages
says she wants to sing for us.
Shoulders back, she begins.
Her eyes are closed as she sends out the song.
I want to listen, but she is moving now –
her, the lectern and the music she is making
rise into the air.
I see no ropes, no pulleys
yet she is up
beyond the curtain fringe.
Then a slice of the stage drops open beneath her
and I gasp as I see what is planned.

Down into the trap room she goes.

I wasn't sure her song fitted
or exactly what she was trying to say
but her poems had me clapping.
I turn to you realising that I don't own her books
or remember her name.
No one in the audience seems the least perturbed;
they are going for ice-cream.

Come on, you say, *they've got three different vegan flavours.*

Jars

It was a surprise
so I kept my eyes closed
all the way to the garden.
My empty stomach
was a kaleidoscope of gems.

She stopped me walking
invited me to open my eyes.

An enormous glass jar
had been delivered to our lawn.
Above it
swinging from a crane
was a lid.

Do you like it? she asked.
It's huge, I managed.
I am going to exhibit you,
she said excitedly. *You like things in jars.*

I did. That was the truth.
A collection of smurfs,
smartie lids, miniature carved owls,
that figure of Dick Tracy.
I liked looking at them
it made dusting easier
they could be handed to someone
with ease, for scrutiny.

I wasn't sure this was right for me.

I ordered an extra-large one,
she was saying.
She seemed to be making a speech,
a declaration of love.
I was supposed to be grateful now,
touched, overwhelmed.

Two men were grinning at me
asking her if I was ready.
Then I was on a platform
being lowered in.

I smiled like a good exhibit should
as the lid was lowered on.
It fitted firmly.

Did she know I'd make condensation?
Would spoil the whole effect?

Gallery 5 – The gallery of finality

Enter to the sound of deathwatch beetles.
Inside you will find:

a selection of black cardigans,
a hotel hand towel,
a patio with a taxidermy pelican posed as if dancing,
a ceramic blackbird,
the skull of a horse,
helicopter rotor blades,
a large plate of soul cakes at the centre of a buffet table.

Deathwatch Beetles

She heard them last night
ticking like a metronome
counting the minutes
in tallies of six.

She was sure they were dancing;
feelers high
vibrating the air
sending out invisible ripples
to celebrate an end.

She imagined them
fixed on the trickle
of sand
falling through life's timer;
exhilarated
by that final rush of grains.

Overnight

You have changed the font
of all the funeral parlour names
to comic sans.

You have taken every lightbulb
from the amber of the traffic lights.

You have abandoned wet, black cardigans
in the middle of roads
to be dead black cats
catching my eye
before the sun splits the sky in two.

You have made all autumn leaves
still clinging to the trees
only sour yellow.

You have torn each dropped leaf.

Where I slow for the final roundabout
you have left me one small, dead cat
a momentary discarded cardigan;
its body curled as if sleeping.

Do Geese See God?

You dry your eyeballs on a hotel hand towel
to remind yourself it hurts.

The head cannot tell the heart how it feels and
there are too many questions without answers.

You can't even bring yourself to slip cream in your
coffee.

If she poured it in for you,
would you take it?

Air hardly enters this room
because hotel windows do not trust you not to jump.

You desire the guillotine of a sash window – no wedges,
no disclaimers,
because hotel windows do not trust you not to jump.

Air hardly enters this room,
would you take it if she poured it in for you?
You can't even bring yourself to slip cream in your
coffee.

Without answers; there are too many questions.
The head cannot tell the heart how it feels and
to remind yourself it hurts,
you dry your eyeballs on a hotel hand towel.

A Pelican is Dancing on the Patio

And there is a disco
very deep in the woods.

The pelican is tapping out its rhythm
and no one can quite name the tune
even though it is right there
on the tip of tongues.

And the people that know about the disco
very deep in the woods
are glad they are not there
under the lights and rotor blades.

The pelican
is making quite some draught now
its wings high and flapping.
It turns in circles
ecstatic in its dance.

And the people that know about the disco
very deep in the woods are checking
on their loved ones
and they are desperately trying to name
what that bird is dancing to.

Blackbird

On my doorstep a blackbird.

A plump bundle
tied with one flat, black shoelace.

Its beak opens and closes mournfully
as I stare at its silence.
It rolls onto its back, offers me its feet.

Summoned to this carefully laced parcel
by knuckle rap against glass
I stand glad
that she has not varnished its beak shut.

I have seen raw chicken breasts tied with string.
Stuffed first with fried onion, cubed pink ham,
tarragon and cream.
Watched fat
bubble from flesh
in a hot oven.
Seen the string tighten
demanding scissoring before serving
to expose criss-cross scars
that I covered with spoonfuls of sauce.

This bird would be lighter than that breast,
if I picked it up; its swell all air
an old balloon in my hands.

I watch my blackbird
wonder how long its wings have been still.
Shouldn't it be fighting back?

If I cut it free, would it fly?
Is there still a song inside?

I've Nothing to Offer the White Horse in the Dream

Head down shy
a white horse senses me,
whinnies – as if a desire to gallop
is rising inside.

She comes right up to the fence.

Spider-leg eyelashes frame her eyes,
defined jawbone
makes her almost too thin.

I want to touch
the coarse hair of her mane
to know if her blood warms it.

I am wishing now for an apple
or a carrot.

As if reading my mind her mouth opens,
those pupils flash wild.

I have nothing to offer.

A cloud of hayed breath
puffs between us.
Before I can release myself from her gaze
she clamps my arm.

When I was young
I used to bite my forearms
to feel the resistance of flesh
imprint my incisors.

I bit my brother once.

Now there is a horse,
with blunted yellowed teeth,
latched on hard, biting my skin to burst it

to taste the metal of my blood.

Do You Hear the Helicopters?

Are they putting their rotor blade
throb in your chest?

Are you amazed at how much space
your ribcage has for this sound?

Are they making your neck ache
as you squint for the pilot?

Are you scared they're not going to drop
a line for you?

Would you like to be held
just dangling before being reeled in?

Can you feel the exhilaration
of the straight up ride?

Do you think they are now turning
into over-sized bees?

Can you name this feeling?

When I Am Gone

serve soul cakes.

Sprinkle dried green lettuce
on salty crackers
plate up purple and orange macaroons
yellow too if it pleases you.

Spear black olives onto cocktail sticks
put out far too many bottles of red wine.

Spend an hour of your morning
cracking almonds into small bowls
sweep up the debris with your hands.
Let each fruit be a memory
but watch out for the bitter ones.

Everything should fit mouths
that are not hinged to be wide
have potential to be slipped in
nonchalantly between tales
that bring out hard laughter.

Except apples.
They will let you watch for:
who bites right in
who takes a knife to them
who puts two in their bag for later.

At the end
if a soul cake remains on that table
take it to the coast.

Await the interest of gulls
then toss it decidedly upwards.

Let the cries fill the air.

As you enter the corridor, follow the signs to our Gift Shop. Please note the display case of several unexhibited artefacts as you pass.

Museum of a Life: The Unexhibited

The bath where she was made to wash by her first lover.
The shower where she was lime-soaped by her second.
An unwritten postcard from Herm where she floated in the bay laughing with her third.

Dinner plate of sliced tomatoes kaleidoscoped with red onion rounds, drizzled in olive oil. Photo, France.
A white bread roll. Origin, Las Vegas.
Barcelona street map displayed here in the front pocket of the rucksack she wore against her breasts to minimise the risk from pickpockets.

The green carnation, and the 'fucking hostile' badge from the blind date with the woman who went on to become her wife.
The stars she couldn't believe she saw when she tipped the bucket chair back, fell and hit her head.
The missed beat from the intro to the first dance at her wedding.

60-watt lightbulb previously inserted into her mouth while she pretended to be a lamp on a car journey back from Whitstable.
The orgasm she had while watching Wendy James from the edge of the stage, Hammersmith Odeon, 1989.

Yellow sailing trousers and blue t-shirt from the Saturday night disco at Manchester Pride (year unrecorded).

The kitchen counter she leant on to tell her mum she was gay.
Her mum, who already knew, who had done for years, and wondered why she hadn't said it herself sooner.
Snakebite and black from the bottom of her boots the night she danced with Chris's girlfriend.

Two Dolly Parton backstage passes and associated Meet and Greet photos.
A jar of Smurfs.
Ronnie (cuddly toy and photogenic alter ego) purchased Chester Zoo, 2002.

Black velvet smoking jacket and size 10 jeans.

*Please exit via the **Gift Shop**
for souvenirs of your visit to this museum.*

Items on sale include:

*dog blankets
packets of wrapped mints
blue apples,
inflatable ladders
wind-up plastic pelicans
tea towels
and postcards.*

*We hope you enjoyed the museum and that you will come
again. Please tell all your friends and family of our exhibits.*

Acknowledgements

My thanks to the editors of the following print and online journals who have published some of the poems in this collection with the same or modified version of the text:

Apex: 'Hanging On'.
Apex: 'Last Night I Dreamt I Slid My Poems into Drawers of Disinfectant to Sterilise Their Titles.
Dear Reader: 'Acceleration'.
Dear Reader: 'A Garden Pond'.
Dear Reader: 'An Apple for My Mum'.
Dear Reader: 'Invitation'.
Dear Reader: 'When I Am Gone'.
Fevers of the Mind: 'The Peacock'.
Fevers of the Mind: 'When I Saw Jesus in a Tomato'.
Ink Sweat and Tears: 'A Pelican is Dancing on the Patio'.
Ink, Sweat and Tears: 'Blade'.
Ink, Sweat and Tears: 'Clambake'.
Ink, Sweat and Tears: 'Skating'.
'The Interpreter's House: 'Do Geese See God'.
One Hand Clapping: 'Hopscotch'.
One Hand Clapping: 'Jars'.
One Hand Clapping: 'Silence'.
Out on the Page: 'Museum of a Life'.
Rough Diamond: 'Tuesday Night'.
The Broken Spine: 'I Hate You'.
The Trawler: 'Overnight'.
The Trawler: 'The Coin'.
Yaffle Press: 'Rescuing the Giraffe'.

192 Poets Directory: 'We Few Deified We Few'.

My thanks also to Damien Donnelly for the many opportunities to share readings of my poems on the poetry podcast '*Eat the Storms*', and for making five o'clock on a Saturday afternoon tea and cake time.

And to Josephine Lay for her keen editing and good humour, which helped me finalise and polish this collection.

Sue Finch likes all kinds of coasts, peculiar things, and the scent of ice-cream freezers. She lives with her wife in North Wales.

Her first published poem appeared in *A New Manchester Alphabet* in 2015 whilst studying for her MA with Manchester Metropolitan University. She won second prize in the 'Wild Words Single Poem Contest' in 2020 with *Flamingo*, a poem which then went on to be included in her debut collection, *Magnifying Glass*, and to be recorded for iamb. She was nominated for a Pushcart Prize in 2022 by Black Bough Poetry, and nominated for Best of the Net in 2023 by The Broken Spine.

Her work has appeared in a number of online magazines including: The Interpreter's House, Ink, Sweat and Tears, Dear Reader, One Hand Clapping and IceFloe Press.

This is her second collection with Black Eyes and takes its title from the poem, *Museum of a Life*. The poem itself was originally selected for publication in the anthology, 'Queer Writing for a Brave New World' published by Out on the Page and is based on the idea of a person's life being exhibited for others to see. Each gallery in this book is themed and features carefully curated exhibits for the reader to peruse. There is a chronology to the different displays leading from a child falling into a pond to an adult contemplation of the preparation of a funeral buffet. Gallery 4 features poems formed from pandemic dreams and nightmares.

Full Quotes

'Sue Finch's voice is both steady and questioning as she sets down the archive of her life museum and invites you to lean in for a closer look. Each exhibit feels like a very personal and off-kilter chronicle of a collective memory where wolves and silence stand with their backs to the corners of the theatrical space of a museum cabinet in which Smurfs and giraffes have walk-on parts. And it's well worth imagining the gift shop – that unsettling pelican's disco moves stencilled on a tea towel; a postcard steeped in the metal taste of the narrator's own blood.'

Helen Ivory.

'Ponds, pitfalls, pandemics, peacocks, pelicans and funeral preparations. On view in Sue Finch's second collection is a kaleidoscope of memory, moments, fears and desires, curated in a lyrical museum with spotlights on circus tents, taxidermy tables, distant dreams and swirling nightmares. The recollections are residues on the tip of the tongue, the names of each already faded, fallen or pulled like the pelt from the flesh with only a metallic tang left in its wake and the future is a disco very deep in the woods with tunes yet to be identified. This is a Daliesque ramble through the gardens of life, an asymmetrical, syncopated joyride. Welcome to the Museum of a Life is triumphant with its directions, distractions and dancing Deathwatch Beetles. Buy a ticket in advance to spare yourself the disappointment of this museum being sold out!'

Damien B Donnelly.

'At once mindful and surreal, these poems take us on a journey through the Museum of a Life, passing from childhood, through vivid everyday events, to love and dreams, and to considerations of mortality. The intriguing exhibits include the small but profound miracle of a tortoise waking from hibernation, the revelation of night skies in the armpits of a lover, a poet rescuing a giraffe after an earthquake, a dancing pelican and other such wonders. Like all the best museums, this one does not have too many rules, and we can walk amongst and interact with the poems at will. Sue Finch welcomes us into a world of multisensory surround sound. Unsentimental yet tender, this collection is an original and imaginative celebration of the temporary treasures of life, and of the human condition.'

Ivor Daniel.

www.ingramcontent.com/pod-product-compliance
Lightning Source LLC
Chambersburg PA
CBHW041313110526
44591CB00022B/2901